SURVIVAL SKILLS HANDBOOK

EXPEDITION PLANNING

Bear Grylls

This survival skills handbook was specially put together to help young explorers like you to stay safe in the world. An expedition is an adventure which allows you to experience the natural world in a wonderful and powerful way, but the success of any adventure relies on careful planning beforehand. This book will teach you what to take with you, how to create a camp, and how to avoid dangers when out exploring the wild. Above all, it is here to help you fully enjoy the adventure!

Bear

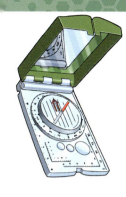

CONTENTS

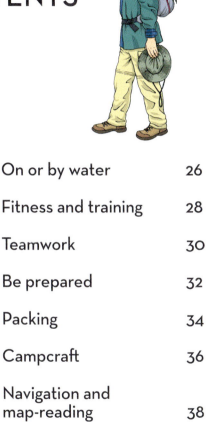

AIMS AND OBJECTIVES

Before starting out, it's a good idea to plan out your aims and objectives... Sit down with your team beforehand and decide what you want to achieve – whether it's a new challenge, exploring a new place, or just a fun adventure in the wild.

Why go on an expedition?

An expedition is an extended journey through the wild. It probably won't be easy and may well have some tough moments. So why do it? Here are some of the benefits of going on an expedition:

- Fun and adventure in new surroundings.
- Explore the natural world.
- Learn new skills such as fire-lighting and navigation.
- Be part of a team, and develop leadership skills.
- Challenge yourself and boost your confidence.
- Help a community in need.
- Raise funds for a cause close to your heart.

Location

First, you will need to decide on the location. Some expeditions visit remote, far-away places, while others explore closer to home. Whatever your plans, you need to research your destination carefully, to find out what conditions might be and what you will need to bring.

Planning

The success of any expedition depends on careful planning. This includes travel to and from your destination. Plan your trip in three stages: the journey there, the expedition itself, and the return home.

Type of expedition

How will you explore? There are many different methods of travel. Many expeditions involve several types.

BEAR SAYS

Take time to plan all aspects of your expedition. How big is your team? How long will the trip last? Maybe don't be overly ambitious on your first attempt!

horse riding

canoeing or kayaking

cycling

CLOTHING

Having the right gear is crucial to the success of any expedition. Finding out about climate and conditions in advance is very important, as this will help you decide what to pack. The clothes, footwear, and kit you will need might vary a lot depending on the weather and terrain of the area you're exploring.

Expedition gear

This picture shows basic clothing for an expedition. It's best to prepare for all sorts of weather. Expeditions to extreme environments may involve special kit (see pages 16-17).

Layer method

Wear several light layers to keep comfortable in changing conditions. Each layer traps warm air. Peel off a layer if you get too hot, and add a layer if you feel cold.

snow goggles

woolly or sun hat

scarf or bandana

layers of clothing

gloves

water- and wind-proof jacket

waterproof trousers

hiking boots

base layer traps warm air next to your skin

mid layer

outer layer and waterproof shell

Things to remember

Clothing should be loose-fitting and comfortable. Avoid jeans as they soak up water if it rains.

gloves or mittens will help keep your hands warm

a first aid kit including suncream is vital

hats are a must for all expeditions – pack a sun, rain, or woolly hat depending on the weather forecast

BEAR SAYS

Pack spare clothes in a waterproof bag to keep them dry. If your boots get wet, pack them with newspaper and put them in a warm place to dry out.

Footwear

A pair of stout shoes or boots are vital when hiking. Make sure your boots are well "broken in" but not too worn. Clean and waterproof your footwear. Hiking socks help to prevent blisters. You may need lightweight shoes for around camp as well.

wear your boots to "break them in" before an expedition to avoid blisters and make sure they are comfortable to hike in

hiking socks will help protect your feet and keep them warm

carrying a tin of boot wax will allow you to keep your boots waterproofed and in good condition

SHELTER

Most trips that last more than one day will involve at least some camping. A good-quality tent, sleeping bag, and mat will keep you dry and comfortable overnight.

Tents

Your tent is your base and home. It also protects you from the elements. Tents come in many shapes and sizes. Your choice will depend on group size and the conditions you are likely to experience.

dome tents are easy to erect but can be tricky to take down and pack away

ridge tents are built around an A-frame and are very sturdy but can be bulky to carry

BEAR SAYS

Practise putting up and taking down your tent, including in windy conditions. Use a mallet to hammer in tent pegs securely and make sure the ropes are taut.

tube tents provide extra room for storage

Sleeping mats

Sleeping on the ground can be pretty uncomfortable. Luckily, there are several different types of sleeping mat or camp bed you can use to provide comfort and insulate you from the cold and wet ground, ensuring a good night's sleep!

camp beds are comfy
but heavy to carry

camping mats are basic, but are lightweight and easy to carry (in the military we used to cut the roll mat down so that it took up less space in our packs. We would cut it down to just cover our top half which is the key part of the body, the core, to keep warm).

a camping mattress can be packed up very small and inflated using a small foot or hand pump

Sleeping bags

A good sleeping bag will keep you cosy overnight, and is one of the most important pieces of kit for any expedition. Research different types of sleeping bag before you go, so you have the right one for your trip.

sheet sleeping bags
are good for hot
climates and if you're
sleeping in hostels

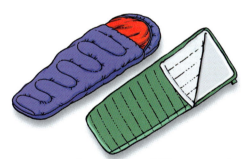

there are plenty of different types of sleeping bag to choose from – do your research beforehand to pick the correct bag for the correct environment

stuffing a jumper inside
your sleeping bag case
will make a good pillow

FOOD, WATER, AND COOKING

Food and water provide the fuel you need to stay active, fit, and healthy. Hot food and or drink are a must after a long, cold day's hike, and will also help to boost your spirits. You may be able to buy or find food as you go along, but you should always bring supplies with you.

Expedition supplies

You need a lot of stores for a multi-day expedition. Plan a detailed menu so you take the right ingredients. All team members should lend a hand with cooking. Dried foods and canned foods will keep for a long time, though canned foods can be quite heavy.

BEAR SAYS

Store foods in a dry place, out of reach of animals such as mice, rats, raccoons, and bears. Hanging food high up in trees is the best bet. Use paracord.

Food pyramid

A balanced diet is vital to keep expedition members healthy. You need a varied diet containing carbohydrates, protein, fruit and vegetables, vitamins, and minerals every day. You also need fats, but avoid too much fatty and sugary food.

limit red meat, butter, and fatty and sugary foods

1–2 servings dairy

1–2 servings protein (eggs, fish, meat, cheese)

2–3 litres of water

1–2 servings legumes, nuts, and seeds

5–8 servings whole grains

3–4 servings plant oils and healthy fats

4–5 servings vegetables

4–5 servings fruit

Trail snacks

Trail snacks provide energy while you're on the move. Sugary snacks can provide short bursts of energy, but it is better to go for foods like fruit, nuts, and protein-based snack bars.

Local foods

Most expeditions use local foods to add to their stores. You can also forage for wild foods, but you need to be absolutely sure to identify the right species, as some plants and many fungi contain deadly poison.

Drinking water

You need to drink at least 2-3 litres of water a day – more if you are active or in a hot climate. You will need to purify all water sourced from the wild, so bringing water purification tablets or iodine drops with you is a good idea.

Stoves and cooking kit

Stoves use different fuels, such as gas, paraffin, or solid fuel. You may be able to cook over your campfire. Your cooking kit should include matches, pots and pans, chopping board and knife, wooden spoon, and spatula, plus mug, bowl, plate, and cutlery. Always wash them thoroughly after use.

HEALTH AND FIRST AID

It is vital that all expedition members have at least a basic knowledge of first aid. Go on a first aid course and practise basic techniques before setting off on a major trip. Make sure you know any medical needs of expedition members in advance, and mark all medications clearly.

First aid kit

Pack a full first aid kit, including bandages, dressings, plasters, tape, scissors, tweezers, and disposable gloves.

First aid drill

In the event of an accident, keep calm and assess the situation. Get everyone out of danger, assess the injury, and contact the emergency services straight away if possible.

Emergency ABC

If an accident strikes remember ABC – Airway, Breathing, Circulation.

First, talk to the patient to see if they are conscious. Shout if needed. If they don't respond:

A. Tilt their head back to clear their **airway**. Make sure nothing is lodged in their throat.
B. Check to see if the patient is **breathing**. Is their chest rising? Hold a mirror under their nose to see if their breath fogs it up.
C. Check their **circulation** by checking their wrist or neck for a pulse.

BEAR SAYS

Wash your hands thoroughly before treating an injury. Wear disposable gloves, especially when treating open wounds such as cuts and burns.

Recovery position

Place an unconscious patient in the recovery position to keep their airway clear and avoid further injury. Roll them onto their side. Bend their upper arm under the lower cheek and place their upper leg at right-angles to their body.

Cuts

Wash the affected area thoroughly to avoid dirt getting into the wound and causing an infection. Press a cloth or dressing on the wound to staunch the bleeding, then cover the wound with a plaster or clean dressing.

Bites and stings

If the sting is left in the wound, carefully remove it with tweezers. Wash the wound site and cover with an iced or cold dressing. If necessary, ask an adult to provide the patient with painkillers.

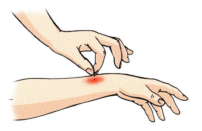

Burns

Run the wound site under cold or lukewarm water. Do not use ice, as this may damage the skin further. Cover the burn with a non-stick dressing, cling-film, or even a clear plastic bag. Ask an adult to provide painkillers if needed.

OTHER KIT

Expeditions require all sorts of gear besides food, camping, and first aid equipment. Think about what you will need during the day, when you camp and overnight.

notebook and pencils

portable GPS

torch

mobile phone in a waterproof case and a portable charger

waterproof matches

compass and map

flint and steel

pen knife

watch

BEAR SAYS

Read through the instructions on all equipment. Practise to make sure you know how to use your kit.

whistle

backpack

Emergency shelter

A rope or paracord and tarpaulin will help you to rig an emergency shelter any time, anywhere.

Repair kit

A needle and thread, clear tape, plastic tape, safety pins, elastic bands, and superglue will help you mend tears and rips to clothing, maps, tents and other gear.

Personal kit

A washbag should contain personal items such as soap, shampoo, toothbrush, and toothpaste. Hygiene is very important on an expedition to avoid getting sick or an infection. Don't forget suncream and lip salve to protect your skin from the sun.

personal kit, lip balm, suncream

Extras

Consider taking these extras, but don't let your pack get too heavy!

playing cards

binoculars

camera

WOODS AND FORESTS

Do your homework before setting out on an expedition. Study maps of the region. Find about about climate, wild foods, natural hazards, and dangerous animals. Woods and forests offer sheltered conditions, but route-finding is difficult.

Navigation

Navigation is tricky in woods and forests because you can't see the way ahead. Dense vegetation can hide hazards such as sheer cliffs and deep gorges. Check the map for landmarks such as rivers, bridges, buildings, and settlements. Take advantage of clearings and high ground to scout the area ahead.

Finding your way

It's hard to move in a straight line through woodland. In fact, it's all too easy to go round in a big circle! Use a compass bearing (see pages 40-41) to head in the right direction. Send one person ahead in that direction, then have them stop before they go out of sight. Join them and repeat.

Communication

All members of the party should carry a whistle so you can communicate if out of sight. Work out some simple signals everyone knows, for example five whistle blasts means return to base.

Dangerous animals

Some forests contain predators such as wolves and bears. Suspend food on a rope looped over a high branch to avoid attracting bears and other scavengers.

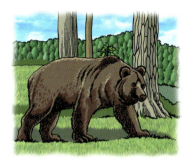

Build a debris shelter

1. Wedge a long, straight branch against a tree-trunk or in a tree-fork to make a ridgepole.
2. Lay smaller branches against it to create a tent shape.
3. Weave twigs, leaves, and debris between the branches to provide shelter from wind and rain.

BEAR SAYS

Wild foods such as nuts and berries may be found in woods and forests, but great care is needed to identify them, as they may be deadly.

DESERTS AND DRY PLACES

Less than 25 cm of rain falls each year in a desert, creating a very dry, often very hot environment. Very few plants and animals can survive in deserts, meaning that food, water, and shelter can be very difficult to come by.

Save water

Water is the body's main need. You cannot survive for more than a few days without it. Make sure you have adequate water supplies before venturing into a desert. Conserve water by resting in the shade by day and working or travelling at night.

Finding water

Study your map for likely water sources. Oases form where underground water seeps to the surface. You can also fill water tanks at wells. A dried-up river bed may hold water if you dig below the surface. Plants growing on a cliff will be watered by a spring or seep, so keep an eye out for plant life. It is also possible to find water inside some species of cactus, like the barrel cactus.

BEAR SAYS

If your vehicle breaks down, stay in its shade and wait for another vehicle to pass. Don't head off into the desert.

Climate and clothing

Deserts have extreme temperatures – scorching hot by day, freezing cold at night. Wear lightweight, loose-fitting clothes. Most people who live in the desert wear black, as it expels heat from your body. Light colours will absorb less heat, but will not reflect it as well.

a broad-brimmed hat or head cloth protects your head and the back of your neck from the burning sun

long-sleeved shirts and trousers protect against sunburn

Poisonous animals

Dangerous desert animals include venomous snakes and scorpions. A scorpion's tail is tipped with a painful sting.

boots guard against snakes and scorpions – don't wear flimsy sandals!

Building a desert scrape
1. Dig a pit long and deep enough to lie down in.
2. Cover with a tarpaulin. Weigh the edges down with stones.
3. A double layer of cloth will keep the air cooler below.

JUNGLE AND TROPICS

Jungles are among the toughest environments on Earth. Torrential rain falls almost daily, and these dense, dark forests teem with creepy crawlies. Travel is incredibly difficult, except by river.

Navigation

Route-finding is tricky in the rainforest. Keep to the trail if there is one – people have got lost after taking just a few steps off the track. If there is no trail you might have to hack one with a machete, using your compass to keep on course.

BEAR SAYS

Progress will be very slow if you are hacking your way with a machete. Plan to cover just a short distance each day.

Climate

Over 200 cm of rain falls each year in a rainforest. Thunderstorms strike on most days, and flooding is a danger in the rainy season.

Kit and clothing
- Wear a long-sleeved shirt and trousers to guard against biting insects.
- A wide-brimmed hat will keep the sun off.
- High boots protect against leeches when crossing streams.
- Essential kit includes a machete, compass, GPS, and mosquito net.

Wildlife
Large mammals such as elephants and rhinos live in rainforests. Tigers and jaguars are top predators. Many snakes, frogs, spiders, and centipedes are armed with poison, while leeches, ticks, and vampire bats will suck your blood.

Jungle bivouac
1. String a rope between two trees at head height and tighten until taut.
2. Throw a tarp over the rope and peg the ends securely.
3. Now rig a hammock or camp bed at waist height, out of reach of creepy crawlies.

BEAR SAYS
Bugs and germs breed quickly in the tropics. Make sure all wounds are sterilized and take extra care to purify your water.

COLD PLACES

Expeditions to the tundra and polar regions face a tough survival challenge. Storms, ice-covered lakes, and predators are serious hazards, while hypothermia and frostbite can strike quickly in icy conditions.

Climate

The polar regions are the coldest places on Earth. Temperatures only rise a few degrees above freezing in summer and can drop to -40°C in winter. Strong winds make the air seem even colder. It's light for 24 hours a day in summer, and dark all day in winter.

Cold-weather hazards

Hypothermia is when your body temperature drops dangerously low. Hot food or drinks will help you recover. Frostbite is when the skin starts to freeze. Check the nose, ears, fingers, and toes for signs of frostbite.

Kit and clothing

Wear several layers of warm clothing including thermal underwear. The outer layer should be wind- and waterproof trousers and jacket with a warm hood. Goggles prevent snow blindness. You may also need snow shoes, a snow shovel, GPS, and emergency flares.

frostbite

Blizzards

In a blizzard, whirling snow fills the air, and visibility falls to zero. Don't try to travel when the weather's like this. Stay in your tent, but go outside regularly to clear heavy snow from the fabric, or the tent could collapse under the weight.

Predators

Polar bears live in the High Arctic and are among the most dangerous animals on Earth, so should be avoided. If you are in an area where polar bears are common, it might be worth hiring an armed guard. Grizzly bears also hunt on the tundra, while walruses and huge elephant seals live on polar coasts.

Snow trench shelter

1. Dig a long snow trench about 0.5 m deep.
2. Excavate the snow in blocks about 40 x 50 cm and 15 cm thick.
3. Lean the blocks together to form a pitched roof over the trench.

BEAR SAYS

Snow-covered landscapes have very few landmarks, so route-finding is difficult. Use a compass to avoid going round in circles.

HILLS AND MOUNTAINS

Mountains have a harsh, cold climate with rapidly changing conditions. The weather can change from baking hot to freezing wind with very little warning. Hazards include glaciers, avalanches, landslides, scree, mist, and fog.

Climate

The temperature drops 1°C for every 150 m you climb. The air high on mountains also contains less oxygen. Above 8,000 m, there is so little oxygen that the body can't survive for long – this region is known as the Death Zone. If you spend time in these conditions, you may suffer from an illness called "altitude sickness", which can be deadly. This can strike at much lower elevations as well. if in doubt, descend.

Kit and clothing

Wear several layers of warm clothing to guard against hypothermia. Goggles and a wool or fleece hat are essential. Climbing gear includes ice axe, harness, rope, and crampons – metal spikes fixed to your boots. Skis, ski poles, and an avalanche probe might come in handy too.

climbing helmet

wool hat or bandana

anti-glare sunglasses, and a spare pair

ski goggles

thin and thick gloves, and a spare pair

climbing harness and rope

ice axes

layers of warm and waterproof clothing

climbing boots with crampons

Mountain camps

Finding a place to camp on a mountain can be difficult. Climbers will bivouac on sleep slopes, dips, and saddles, often having to hack out a small area of flat ground to make camp. Beware avalanche slopes above and always avoid camping in such dangerous zones.

Glaciers

These are masses of ice that carve out valleys through the mountains and slowly flow downhill. They are intercut by deep cracks called crevasses. You have to take special care not to fall into these, especially if the cracks are covered by fresh snow.

Avalanches

An avalanche is when a mass of snow breaks away and thunders downhill, often with terrifying speed. Avalanches can be triggered by the sun's heat or by a climber or skier. The key with avalanche survival is simply to avoid being in a high avalanche situation. If you are caught in an avalanche, use a swimming motion, and fight to stay near the surface. Cover your nose and mouth to avoid inhaling powder snow. When it stops, act fast, and try to kick or claw your way out. Spit to see which way it falls to make sure you are digging in the correct direction, as an avalanche can be very disorientating.

Building a snow hole bivouac

Dig a snow hole in a deep bank of snow. The entrance tunnel should slope down, then upwards, so the cold air will sink. Use a stick or ski pole to make an air hole, and build a sleeping platform.

BEAR SAYS

If thick mist descends, you will need to use your compass to find the way. If you have a GPS device, use it to locate your exact position.

ON OR BY WATER

Many expeditions travel by water and camp by rivers, lakes, or on seashores. This is often a useful method of travel, especially in thick jungle or places where the terrain is harsh. However, these watery places hold their own dangers such as strong currents, tides, rapids, and floods.

Kit and clothing

Canoeists and sailors need specialist kit and clothing. You will need wind- and waterproof gear or a wetsuit, plus a lifejacket and safety helmet.

Capsize drill

All canoeists learn the capsize drill, so they know what to do if their craft overturns. If your canoe has a spray deck, pull off the cover and kick your way to the surface. Expert kayakers can roll right over in their canoe, but it takes a lot of practise to be able to do this.

Abandon ship

If you have to abandon ship, keep your clothes on but remove your shoes, as they will weigh you down. Enter the water gradually if possible. Swim away from a sinking ship.

Treading water

Once in the water, inflate your life jacket or grab a floating object. Don't exhaust yourself swimming unless you are near the shore – just tread water to stay afloat. Crossing your hands and feet and keeping your head dry will help you keep warm.

BEAR SAYS

Beware rip tides that flow away from the shore. If caught in one, don't swim against the current but calmly swim across it, until you are out of it.

BEAR SAYS

Beware waves, tides, and currents in the sea and rivers. Never swim alone. On the seashore, make sure you don't get cut off by the tide.

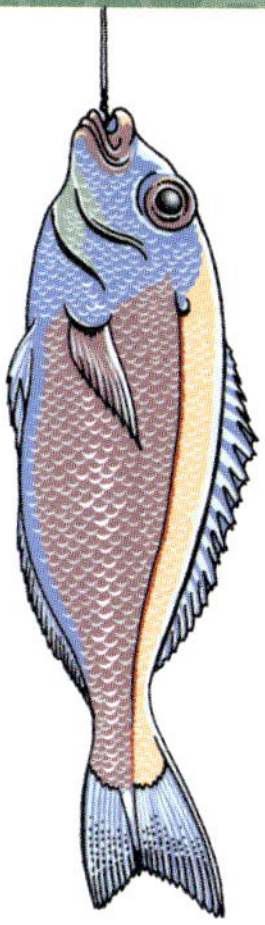

Wild foods

Fresh and saltwater habitats offer foods such as seaweed, fish, and shellfish. You can catch fish with a simple rod and line, but you will need to be very patient. Prepare a fish for cooking by slitting its belly to remove the guts and bones.

Predators

Deadly sea creatures include sharks and poisonous jellyfish, while crocodiles, large snakes, and hippos may lurk in rivers and swamps. Make sure you know what predators are native to the area you are exploring and how to stay safe around them. Don't take chances with crocodiles or hippos – especially in murky water.

River crossing

First, scan the riverbank for the best crossing place. Cross using a stout stick for support, or link arms and cross in groups of two or three. Use any flotation you can find. If in doubt, do not enter rivers. They are incredibly dangerous even when apparently slow moving.

Build a raft

You can make a raft using lengths of bamboo lashed together with cord. Tie crosspieces to make the craft more stable. Two layers of bamboo will make the raft float better. Make paddles out of wood or bamboo.

FITNESS AND TRAINING

You need to be fit for an expedition. Increase your general fitness by taking regular exercise. You will also need to train for any specific activities your trip involves, such as hiking, cycling, climbing, or canoeing.

Fitness routine

Get in good shape through well-planned fitness training. Aim to do half an hour's exercise at least four days a week. If you are unfit, start with lower intensity exercise and build up. This could include time spent doing sport or playing games, gym, dance, brisk walking, or chores such as housework or gardening.

Aerobic exercise

Aerobic means "with oxygen", and includes any exercise that will make your heart and lungs work harder. Aerobic activities, such as jogging, cycling, swimming, or rowing, will improve your stamina over sustained times.

Keeping records

Keep a record of your training. Time yourself over a distance using a stopwatch, or count the number of times you can do an exercise within a specific time such as a minute. Aim to improve your time or increase the intensity and number of exercises you do every week.

Strength and flexibility

Strength exercises such as sit-ups, pull-ups, and press-ups help to build general muscle strength, while stretching exercises make you supple. This will help with any physical activity, but especially activities that require specific muscle groups like cycling, climbing, or canoeing.

Practice makes perfect

You should always practise the specific activity involved in your trip beforehand, in order to build strength and stamina. If your trip will involve covering a certain distance every day, start with a shorter distance in your training, then build up to the distance you will need to do.

Warm up and cool down

It is important to warm up and cool down before and after training by doing stretching exercises, otherwise you may risk damaging your muscles.

✘ BEAR SAYS

Plan gradually and steadily to increase the intensity of your training. Don't go too hard too soon, or you could strain a muscle.

TEAMWORK

Some explorers like to go it alone, but most expeditions involve a whole team of people with a range of different strengths and skills. Not only is going in a group much safer, it offers you the chance to share your adventure and have more fun!

Leadership

Most expeditions are led by one person, though you can also decide to take it in turns to be leader. Being a team leader is rewarding, but also brings responsibility. You are in charge of safety and the smooth running of the expedition, and may need to keep up people's morale. A good leader will make use of people's different talents and will always help those who are struggling.

Pros and cons
Group expeditions have many advantages:
- Safety in numbers.
- Several brains to share decisions such as route-finding.
- Sharing kit such as tents and supplies reduces costs.
- Companionship and fun.

Everyone in the group has to be willing to play their part and share the chores.

Decision-making

A group leader should be open to everyone's ideas and suggestions, but she or he may also need to make tough decisions that not everyone agrees with. Always explain your decisions to your team and take people's feelings into account.

Being a team player

Being part of a team is a fantastic experience, but may sometimes involve accepting decisions you aren't entirely happy about. It is okay to discuss these things, but sometimes be prepared to compromise. Work together to make the team something you can all be proud of!

Building teamwork

Before you set off, practise the activities involved in the expedition together. This will help you get to know one another and find out about strengths and weaknesses. If things don't go to plan, analyze what went wrong. How could the team improve its performance?

Support team

All expeditions should have a backup team which will provide support and may help to solve problems. When setting off on local expeditions, always tell a parent or responsible adult when and where you are going and what time you expect to be back. This means that, if something goes wrong and you do not arrive home, they will be able to send for help.

BE PREPARED

The Scout motto, "Be Prepared", is excellent advice for all expeditions, whether close to home or far away. Plan each stage of the trip carefully in advance, and always make a backup plan in case things go wrong.

Dealing with "red tape"

Foreign and sometimes even local travel involves meeting certain official requirements. If you are travelling abroad, you will need a passport and possibly also a visa. You need tickets and money in the local currency. It is also important to find out in advance if you meet all the medical requirements for the region you are visiting, and have all the vaccinations and medication needed for the trip. For example, many regions will require you to take malaria medication.

Local guides

Many expeditions to remote places hire a local guide to show the way and provide expert advice on wild foods, poisonous plants, and dangerous animals. If you don't hire a guide, you will need to learn at least a few words of the language, research local customs, and find out how people live.

Timetable

Making a timetable will help you plan your adventure. Below is an example of what an expedition timetable may look like.

Day 1. Take the 1600hrs 7a bus from Weston to Smalltown and walk to Campsite 1. ETA (estimated time of arrival): 17.15. Make camp and prepare meal.

2. Day 2. 10 km hike from Campsite 1 to Campsite 2 at Northport. ETA: 1600 hrs. Camp and prepare meal.

Day 3. 11 km hike from Campsite 2 to Campsite 3 at Westport. ETA: 1600 hrs. Camp and prepare meal.

Day 4. Catch 11.00 bus 10a from Westport to Weston, ETA 1200. Walk home.

Emergency plan of action

Even the best-run expeditions don't always go to plan. Try to think about what could go wrong. Write an Emergency Plan of Action (EPA), giving details of what to do if things don't go to plan, for example if the weather is bad or someone gets ill.

EPA information sheet

Your EPA should contain an information sheet for all members of the expedition. This should include their full name and address, passport number, contact details, details of your trip, and contact details for the support team and close family – plus any medical issues. Each member should carry a copy of this. Make sure the EPA is always waterproofed.

PACKING

All expedition members need a rucksack or kit bag to safely stow and carry their gear. You should pack carefully so that you can easily lay your hands on what you need, when you need it. Planning your packing beforehand will save you a lot of time and effort when you are out on your adventure.

Choosing a rucksack
There are several different types of rucksack. If buying one, try it on to see if it feels comfortable.

- Does it have a hip belt and all the features you need?
- Frame or inner-frame rucksacks allow air to circulate between your back and the rucksack, reducing sweat.
- A small daypack can be useful to carry items you need during the day.
- Strong, adjustable hip belt takes the weight off your shoulders.
- A chest strap helps to balance the pack.

Waterproofing
A good rucksack cover will help keep the rain off your rucksack. It's also important to use a waterproof "liner" or plastic bag inside the pack too, to keep the contents dry. You don't want to get to camp after a long day's hike in the rain only to find all your clothes and equipment soaked!

Packing

Storing selected kit in cloth or plastic bags before you pack them will help you find items quickly. Pack your gear in reverse order, so the things you will need first are on top. Put heavy items close to your back to stop them putting extra strain on your shoulders. Vital items such as your first aid kit should be at the very top, so they can be accessed quickly in an emergency.

BEAR SAYS

Carrying too much weight will slow you down and make the journey harder. Be smart and disciplined with both essentials and luxuries.

keep fragile items and things you will need during the day (waterproof, first aid kit) stored at the top

heavy items (such as your tent) should be stored next to your back

items that are only needed at the camp should be stored at the bottom

CAMPCRAFT

All the skills used in outdoor camping are known as campcraft. This includes putting up a tent, lighting a fire, and cooking outdoors. Organize your camp so it is safe, practical, and comfortable for everybody on your expedition.

Camp location

Choose a level spot for your camp, if possible near a source of wood and water. But don't camp in a valley bottom or by a stream or river that could flood after heavy rain. Avoid the banks of lakes where mosquitoes breed.

Organising your camp

choose a place to keep tools and equipment where everybody can find them easily

store food and leftovers out of reach of animals

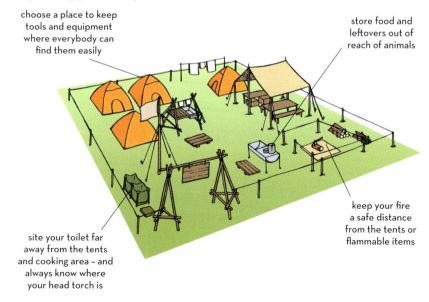

site your toilet far away from the tents and cooking area – and always know where your head torch is

keep your fire a safe distance from the tents or flammable items

Firemaking

To light a campfire, you will need tinder to take the spark, and kindling to fan it. You will also need different sizes of wood to feed the fire. Choose a sheltered location and clear the ground of debris. The easiest way to light a fire is by using matches or a lighter. A fire steel will also strike a spark.

BEAR SAYS

Beware dead branches on mature trees, which could fall on you or your tent. Falling dead branches is a big danger in jungles.

Fire safety

Fires are very dangerous. Make sure you make your fire a safe distance from your tents, and have water standing by so you can put the fire out if necessary. Always make sure your fire is completely out before you move on – you don't want to risk causing damage to the area.

Cooking tripod

You can hang a kettle over the fire using a tripod. You will need three strong, straight sticks of about the same length. Bind rope around one end, then splay the legs out, creating a tripod. Place the tripod over the fire, making sure it is stable, then attach the kettle on a hook.

NAVIGATION AND MAP-READING

Everyone should learn the basics of navigation before setting out on an expedition. One of the most important navigational skills is knowing how to read a map. Explorers visiting unknown regions may draw their own maps for future expeditions.

Maps and symbols

Maps are drawings of the landscape from above, and help us find our way. They use symbols to show landmarks and permanent features such as woods, roads, and rivers. There is normally a "key" or "legend" at the side of the map which explains what the symbols mean.

Scale

Everything on the map is drawn to the same size – this is called the scale. There is a scale bar at the side of the map to show you what scale it is drawn to. For example, 1 cm on the map may represent 0.5 km, 1 km, or 10 km. Studying the scale helps you judge distances and work out how long it will take to walk anywhere.

disabled access

art gallery

cafe

campsite

castle or fort

cycle trail

fishing

garden

golf course

information centre

picnic site

church or cathedral

public toilets

restaraunt

walks or trails

water

birdwatching

1 inch = 1 mile (1:62,500)

```
O     1        2       3       4        5
```

1 cm = 1 km (1:100,000)

```
O  1  2  3  4  5  6  7
```

Grid references

Squares on the map form a grid which can help you pinpoint locations. These are called grid references. To read or give a grid reference, start at the bottom left-hand corner of the map. Run your finger sideways along the map, then up. Remember this order using this phrase: "through the hall then up the stairs". Grid references give the East-West direction first, then the North-South direction.

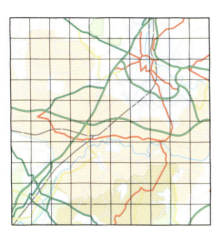

Contour lines

How do you show the ups and downs of the landscape on a flat map? The answer is using contour lines. These lines link places at the same height above sea level. Reading the contours shows you the location of hills and valley, so you know if you have to climb or descend. If the contours are close together, the slope is steep.

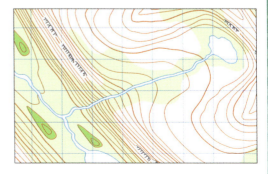

FINDING YOUR WAY

To work out what direction to travel in, you need to know how to use a compass. With a map and compass, you can find your way any time, anywhere! A skilled map-reader can also judge the terrain, distance, and roughly how long a journey will take. The key factors to navigate by are: bearing, distance, time, features, and backdrop (remember this using the words Bear Drinks Tea For Breakfast!)

Parts of a compass

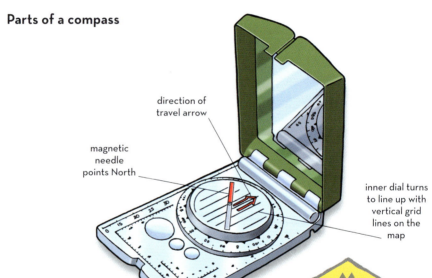

direction of travel arrow

magnetic needle points North

inner dial turns to line up with vertical grid lines on the map

Using a compass

A compass can be used in several different ways to find direction. The red magnetic needle always points North. This allows you to work out the other main compass points: South, East, and West, and all points in between.

⚔ BEAR SAYS

Grid squares on a map can help you judge time and distance. If you walk at 3 km/hr and each square is 1 km, you will walk across roughly three grid squares in an hour at a steady pace.

Orient the map

This process allows you to find your direction with a map and compass.

1. Place the edge of the compass on the map along the route you intend to travel.
2. Turn the inner compass dial so the lines match up with the grid lines on the map. Make sure the red arrow on the dial points to North on the map (usually at the top).
3. Now take the compass off the map and hold it flat. Turn around until the red magnetic needle lines up with the red arrow on the dial. The direction of travel arrow now points to where you want to go.

Judging distance

A device called a map measurer works out distances on a map. Simply run the little wheel along your route and then read the distance. You can also lay a piece of string along your route. Then lay it along the scale bar, several times if necessary, to see how far you have to go.

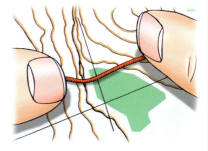

the Southern Cross

the Plough

Navigating by night

If you don't have a compass, you can use the stars to navigate at night. In the Northern Hemisphere the Plough (Great Bear) shows where North is. The two stars on the tip of the Plough point towards Polaris, the North Star. In the Southern Hemisphere, the foot of the Southern Cross points South.

SIGNALLING

Learn to send signals of various kinds before embarking on an expedition. Signalling not only helps the group to stay in contact, but it can also be used to call for help, which could save your life in an emergency.

Two types of signals

There are two main types of signals: visual and audio signals. These correspond with our two main senses, sight and hearing. Visual signals include flags, light flashes, direction arrows, and texts on your mobile. Audio signals include phone calls, shouts, and whistle blasts.

Natural materials

Natural materials can be used to mark a trail. You can also send a distress call by arranging sticks or stones to spell SOS in large letters, or by drawing large letters in mud, snow, or sand.

BEAR SAYS

Distress calls are taken very seriously by the emergency services. Never send out an SOS unless it is a real emergency.

Morse code

This international code uses dots and dashes, or short and long signals, to spell out letters and words. The most important message in Morse code is SOS: three dots, three dashes, and three more dots.

Trail signs

Scouts and Guides use these signs to mark a trail for others to follow.

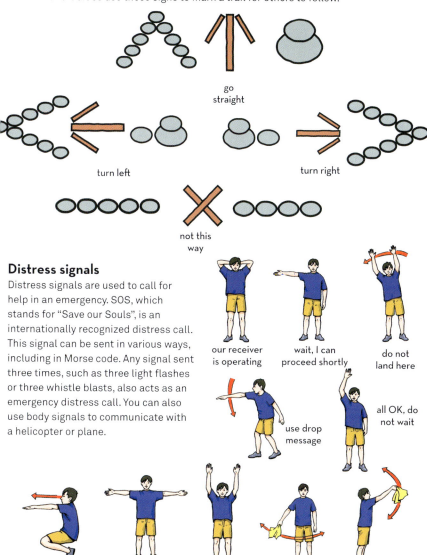

go straight

turn left

turn right

not this way

Distress signals

Distress signals are used to call for help in an emergency. SOS, which stands for "Save our Souls", is an internationally recognized distress call. This signal can be sent in various ways, including in Morse code. Any signal sent three times, such as three light flashes or three whistle blasts, also acts as an emergency distress call. You can also use body signals to communicate with a helicopter or plane.

our receiver is operating

wait, I can proceed shortly

do not land here

use drop message

all OK, do not wait

land here

need mechanical help

pick us up

no

yes

STAYING SAFE

Every expedition will meet with some difficulties or problems. When this happens, the most important thing is to stay calm and work out the best solution. If things don't work out as you hoped, stay positive and switch to your backup plan. It helps to be as flexible as possible. As the Commandos say: comfortable with uncertainty. This is a good trait for the survivor.

Contact base

Make regular contact with your support team at set times, so they know that all is well. This way, if you don't contact them, they will know to send for help. Don't forget to take spare batteries or leads for recharging equipment such as a radio or mobile phones – you don't want to cause an unnecessary panic over a flat battery!

BEAR SAYS

In the event of an emergency, keep cool. Get out of danger, then assess the situation. What are your options? What is the best course of action?

Stay or go?

In a survival situation, one of the most important decisions you will need to make is whether to stay where you are or move on. It is usually safer to stay put. Ask yourself if you will be missed. If so, a search party will almost certainly set out to find you, so it is very important to stay where you are. In a crisis, think about the four basic needs: protection, rescue, water, and food (in that order). If these can be fulfilled, then it's best to stay put.

Moving on

If you are in serious danger, you may need to move. Moving on could also be the best option if no one knows you are missing. If a town or village is in sight, consider going there to ask for help. If you do move on, leave a clear sign, if possible a written note saying who you are, the date and time you left, and where you are headed. Seal the note in a plastic bag to prevent it getting wet or damaged, and leave it in an obvious place, weighted down with a stone.

Lost and found

If you get lost, don't panic. Look around to see if you can spot a landmark such as a road or river to get your bearings. If you have a map, see if you can find the same feature on it, so you can work out your location. If you get separated from your group, it's probably best to stay put and wait for the others to come back and find you.

GLOSSARY

Aerobic exercise – Energetic exercise, such as cycling or jogging, that makes the heart and lungs work harder.

Audio – Relating to sound.

Avalanche – When a mass of snow breaks loose and slips down a mountain.

Avalanche probe – A long pole used to check if snow is firm or if it is likely to come loose and avalanche.

Bearing – The direction in which you are headed, as shown on a compass.

Bivouac – A basic temporary camp. Sometimes shortened to "bivvy".

Cache – A hidden food store, or to store food in a hidden place.

Capsize – When a boat overturns.

Conserve – To save or preserve something.

Contour lines – Lines on a map that show height above sea level.

Debris – Pieces of waste material.

Distress signal – A call for help in an emergency.

Excavate – To dig out or remove loose material such as earth or snow.

Frostbite – Injury to the body caused by extreme cold.

Glacier – A mass of ice that is slowly sliding downhill.

GPS – Global Positioning System. A radio navigation system that allows explorers to see their location.

Grid reference – Numbers referring to the grid squares on a map used to pinpoint locations.

Hypothermia – When the body loses heat in cold temperatures.

Insulate – To keep something warm.

Kindling – Small fuel such as thin sticks, used to feed a newly lit fire.

Morale – Confidence or good spirits.

Morse code – A signalling system made up of long and short signals, also called dots and dashes. Morse code signals can be sent in different ways, for example by flashing a light or blowing a whistle.

Predator – An animal that hunts and kills other animals for food.

Ridgepole – The horizontal pole on a long tent which supports the fabric.

Spray deck – The covering on a kayak which keeps water out of the craft.

Suspend – To hang something, usually in mid-air.

Tarpaulin – A thick waterproof cloth, usually with eyeholes in the corners for attaching. Often called a tarp.

Tinder – Very fine fuel used to catch a spark to light a fire.

Discover more amazing books in the Bear Grylls series:

Perfect for young adventurers, the *Survival Skills* series accompanies an exciting range of colouring and activity books. Curious kids can also learn tips and tricks for almost any extreme situation in *Survival Camp*, explore Earth in *Extreme Planet*, and discover some of history's greatest explorers in the *Epic Adventures* series.

Conceived by Weldon Owen in partnership
with Bear Grylls Ventures

Produced by Weldon Owen, an imprint of Kings Road Publishing
Suite 3.08 The Plaza, 535 Kings Road,
London SW10 0SZ, UK

WELDON OWEN
Editor Susie Rae
Designer Shahid Mahmood
Contributor Jen Green
Illustrator Julian Baker
Cover image © Ben Simms 2018
Printed in Malaysia
2 4 6 8 10 9 7 5 3 1

Disclaimer
Weldon Owen and Bear Grylls take pride in doing our best to get the facts right in putting together the information in this book, but occasionally something slips past our beady eyes. Therefore we make no warranties about the accuracy or completeness of the information in the book and to the maximum extent permitted, we disclaim all liability. Wherever possible, we will endeavour to correct any errors of fact at reprint.

Kids – if you want to try any of the activities in this book, please ask your parents first! Parents – all outdoor activities carry some degree of risk and we recommend that anyone participating in these activities be aware of the risks involved and seek professional instruction and guidance. None of the health/medical information in this book is intended as a substitute for professional medical advice; always seek the advice of a qualified practitioner.

A WELDON OWEN PRODUCTION. AN IMPRINT OF KINGS ROAD PUBLISHING.
PART OF THE BONNIER PUBLISHING GROUP.